ON
THE
EDGE

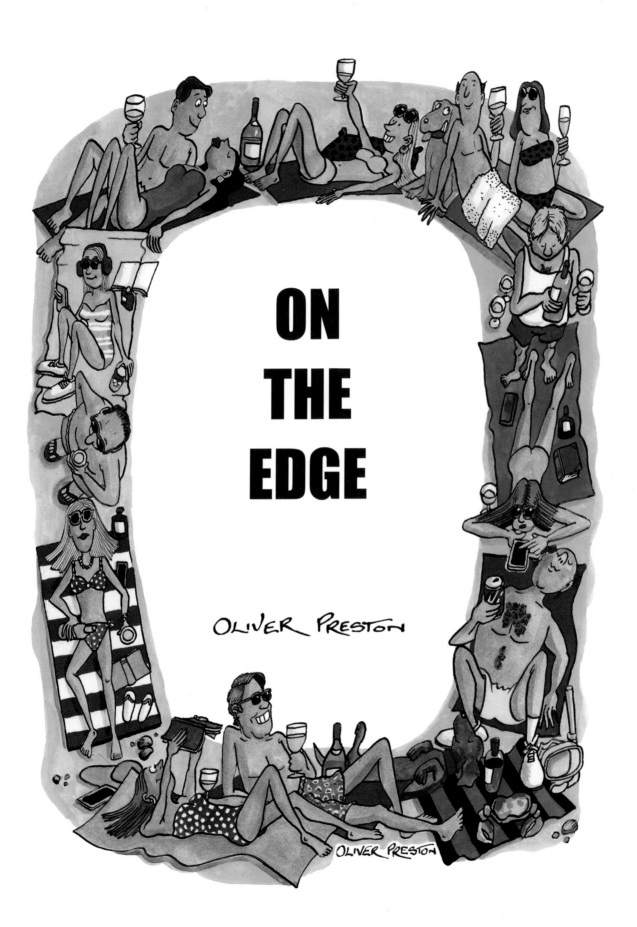

ON THE EDGE

OLIVER PRESTON

For Vivien, Amber and Rex

First published in Great Britain in 2023 by

BEVERSTON PRESS

Tetbury, Glos GL8 8TT

British Library cataloguing in Publication Data
A catalogue record for this title is available from The British Library

ISBN 978-0-9549936-9-6

Designed by Beverston Press Ltd.
Printed by Gutenberg Press, Malta

"When I asked you how you were, I didn't expect you to tell me."

"...and this is my little corner of the garden."

INTRODUCTION

"Good ideas are insistent. Bad ideas leave you alone after a while."

I heard this comment on *BBC* Radio, and it really struck a chord with me. Stored in the plan chests in my studio are many rough sketches that did not quite make the cut for a finished cartoon for publication. I fiddle with captions for my cartoons, but nearly always return to the phraseology of my original idea. The joke that first comes into my head is insistent. When you have only a few seconds to convey a joke to a reader, the caption has to be snappy, the shorter the better, and the joke should arrest the reader's attention, and better still, surprise them with a quirky sense of humour.

I carry a notepad with me, and have to write down ideas and captions as soon as they enter my head. At a meeting, at a dinner, walking on the farm or down a street. On a ski lift. In the bath! If I am driving up to London on the M4 motorway, I often call myself - handsfree - and leave unintelligible, convoluted ideas for cartoons on my answerphone in my studio. My wife, Vivien, is long suffering with my eccentricities. When in the middle of the night I reach out for my notebook, I frequently knock over a glass of water, in a mad effort to inscribe some genesis of a joke. There is no credit for the cartoonist who says, 'I had a great idea last night, but I can't remember what it was'. However, the next day the pencilled scribble, written down in the darkness, is more often than not completely illegible. My wife asks if the spilt water has gone through the ceiling to the room below. But what a reward there is the next day if there is enough of a scribble to remind me of the kernel of a good cartoon idea.

On the Edge is a collection of recent cartoons that cover field sports and skiing, children and schooling, doting dogs and everyday town and country life.   Many of these cartoons were first published in *The Field Magazine* and *Country Life Magazine* and several were drawn for exhibitions in the ski resort of Gstaad. I use a 2B pencil, a gilotte nib pen, black indian ink, coloured inks and gouaches, the same materials I have used for over forty years. When I was 12 my mother gave me some money to buy a set of oil paints to encourage my interest in art, but I couldn't afford the box that I coveted and bought a complete set of Winsor and Newton inks instead. I delved into graphics at school - screen printing and lino cuts - but it was the inks that inspired me, and with a bit of fledgling humour they set me on a path to becoming a cartoonist.

Neil Tennant of *The Pet Shop Boys* commented that, ' the best job you could ever have is making a living out of your hobby.' Drawing and thinking up cartoons has always been my hobby since my school days, so giving humour and smiles, and drawing from my studio in the Cotswolds is a blessing indeed.

OLIVER PRESTON

"Is it safe to join the Ladies?"

"Before you say anything, it wasn't me."

"Stuffed and mounted, please. It's what he would have wanted."

"Video of my husband hitting a pheasant......take twenty-three."

"You should like this bottle. You gave it to us
when you last came to dinner."

"Can you lend me the money to buy you a bottle of Rosé ?"

"Gosh, you look as though you've just paid the school fees."

"...and we'd like our daughter to go to Eton."

"Should we have a post mortem?"

"Has anyone seen my blue trousers?"

"Can she call you back? She's trying out her new skis?"

"Go down on one knee? Are you mad ?
I wouldn't be able to get up again."

"Darling, the spot we got engaged was about three foot to the left."

"...and have any of you lost your sense of taste ?"

"No, THAT'S the scene of the robbery.
This is just my daughter's bedroom."

"The white wine was meant for getting rid
of the red wine stain on the carpet."

"He won't be working from home today. He's not feeling very well."

"You know they EAT rabbits filled with chocolate?"

"We couldn't get a babysitter."

"Daddy, what's wrong with mummy shooting more birds than you ?"

"But you said the cottage was in the middle of nowhere."

"Nice try."

"Not funny, Harry. It's taken me a month."

"Does this look like The Bungalow, 9 Pear Tree Close?"

"Let's finish the last bottle."

"Damn, done for speeding again...."

"I could drop them off in June and pick them up in September."

"Is that the Greengo nightclub? Yes, I'd like to book a table for my son
and his friends. Please put everything on my account."

"I wouldn't mind, but her ski suit cost me an arm and a leg."

"He's been with the family for years."

"Last one to the restaurant pays for lunch."

GSTAAD
"I thought we were lunching at MY club"

OLIVER PRESTON.

"Racing the children down after a good lunch."

"And on the eighth day God created Gstaad."

"Four percent alchohol, ninety-six percent cheese."

"If I let go she'll buy something."

"Do you realise that in twenty years time the country will
be run by people home-schooled by alcholics ?"

"Non-doms have moved in to number 23."

"When dad said speedy boarding, I thought we were taking a plane."

"Can we go Dutch ?"

"Just after losing his service is probably not the best time
to ask my father for my hand in marriage."

"Over."

"Aren't you meant to be in that shoot over there ?"

"Sorry, we forgot to mention the potholes."

"This is the best day ever."

61

"My parents are making way for the younger generation."

"This could be your last chance to get on the housing ladder."

"Margaret, Tony's looking at your cards..."

"Looks like I'm one down."

"We're in Car Park Number One."

"Bridget, that's our horse back there."

"Not ANOTHER box set !"

"Mummy, next time can you practise on the dogs ?"

"Anyway, enough about me. How was your day?"

"Next Step. PUT THE PLATE INTO THE DISHWASHER."

"Nathan, there's a gentleman here trying to pay with his phone."

"Mummy, daddy's hiding wine in the walls again."

"First flower arranging, then art classes, now cookery school.
We're in for a real treat tonight."

'Heavyweight watch collectors promenading through the village.'

"So I told my wife about the new car. Now she wants a new handbag."

GSTAAD
"More horsepower for the village"

"So why did you split up from your last boyfriend ?."

" But darling, the shops were full of things I didn't realise I needed."

"So when did *yours* start becoming woke?"

"And be a darling and get me some tonic."

"Sometimes I think you love pugs more than me."

"I opened the wine to let it breathe but there was no sign of life.
So I had to give it mouth-to-mouth resuscitation."

"Here are my tasting notes."

"...and then I just hit delete."

"...and is your new puppy still chewing your antique furniture?"

"I assume Mary came to clean the house today."

"Lengths, George. Not widths."

"I'll make a cup of tea, if you bring the shopping in from the car."

"She comes for Christmas every year and we have no idea who she is."

...d's holiday from Instagram, Tik Tok, Snapchat, Facebook and Twitter.

ACKNOWLEDGEMENTS

Illustration Acknowledgements

First published

Country Life Magazine: 5, 8, 12, 13,14,16, 22, 24, 26, 29, 30, 32, 33, 34, 36, 38, 41, 43, 52, 54, 55, 56, 58, 60, 62, 64, 66, 69, 70, 72, 74, 77, 80, 82, 84, 85, 86, 88, 90, 92 and 94.
The Field Magazine: 6, 11, 15, 17, 21, 23, 25, 27, 28, 31, 61, 63, 65, 68, 75, 81, and 91.
Gstaad Palace Magazine; 40. **Gstaad My Love Magazine**: 19 and 79.

By the same author

Liquid Limericks (2001)	Robson Books	with Alistair Sampson
Larder Limericks (2004)	Robson Books	with Alistair Sampson
Shall we join the Men (2005)	Beverston Press	
Modern Cautionary Verses (2006)	Constable Robinson	with Charlie Ottley
Hitting the Slopes (2008)	Beverston Press	
How to be Asked Again (2009)	Quiller	with Rosie Nickerson
Out of Town (2010)	Beverston Press	
Out for a Duck (2010)	Quiller	with Ian Valentine
Another Log on the Fire (2011)	Beverston Press	
Real Men Drink Port (2011)	Quiller	with Ben Howkins
Fondue and Furs (2011)	Beverston Press	
Rich Pickings (2013)	Beverston Press	
The Imperfect Shot (2015)	Quiller	with Jeremy Hobson
Lively Limericks (2015)	Beverston Press	with Patrick Holden
Raise Your Game (2016)	Quiller	with Ian Valentine
The Long Weekend (2017)	Beverston Press	
Off Piste (2017)	Beverston Press	
The Dictionary of Posh (2019)	Quiller	with Hugh Kellett

My thanks to Alexandra Henton at the Field Magazine, Mark Hedges and Victoria Marston at Country Life Magazine. To Vivien, Amber and Rex, Baloo and Jazz, for being such a wonderful source of ideas.

Prints and some greeting cards are available from 'On the Edge'.
Visit www.oliverpreston.com or call +44 (0) 1666 502638